MW01440262

A COLORING WONDERLAND FOR MELANIN PRINCESSES

BLACK
GIRL
MAGIC

CURLS
CONFIDENCE
AND
COURAGE

DOPE
BLACK
GIRL

UNAPOLOGETICALLY
Dope

DRIPPING IN
MELANIN

PRETTY
BLACK
and educated

Black Girl
Magic
I SPRINKLE THAT
ON EVERYTHING

BLACK QUEEN
MOST POWERFUL PIECE IN THE GAME

FUTURE LEADER

PRESENT PRINCESS

STRONG
beauty
SMART
powerful
QUEEN

Girl power

She
Believed
so she
did
SUGAR
BABE

POWERED BY THE
BLACK
WOMEN
BEFORE ME

GOOD VIBE
SELF

MELANIN

can't be

BOUGHT

Made in the USA
Columbia, SC
11 July 2024

38359872R00035